To the Extreme

skateboarding

by Matt Doeden

Reading Consultant:
Barbara J. Fox
Reading Specialist
North Carolina State University

Capstone
press

Mankato, Minnesota

Blazers is published by Capstone Press,
151 Good Counsel Drive, P.O. Box 669, Mankato, Minnesota 56002.
www.capstonepress.com

Library of Congress Cataloging-in-Publication Data
Doeden, Matt.
    Skateboarding / by Matt Doeden.
    p. cm.—(Blazers. To the extreme)
    Includes bibliographical references and index.
    ISBN 0-7368-2730-7 (hardcover)
    ISBN 0-7368-5226-3 (paperback)
    1. Skateboarding—Juvenile literature. [1. Skateboarding.
2. Extreme sports.] I. Title II. Series: Doeden, Matt. Blazers.
To the extreme.
GV859.8.D63 2005
796.22—dc22   2003026627

Summary: Describes the sport of skateboarding, including tricks and
    safety information.

Editorial Credits
Angela Kaelberer, editor; Jason Knudson, designer; Jo Miller,
    photo researcher; Eric Kudalis, product planning editor

Photo Credits
Capstone Press/Gary Sundermeyer, 26
Corbis/Duomo, 7, 8, 28–29; NewSport/Al Fuchs, 5, 12; NewSport/
    Rick Rickman, 25; NewSport/X Games IX/Matt A.Brown, 19
Getty Images/Elsa, 11, 20 (left), 22; Ezra Shaw, cover, 23;
    Stanley Chou, 13, 21 (right)
Index Stock Imagery/Barry Winiker, 16–17
Mira/Carl Schneider, 20–21; Mira/Todd Powell Photography, 15

Table of Contents

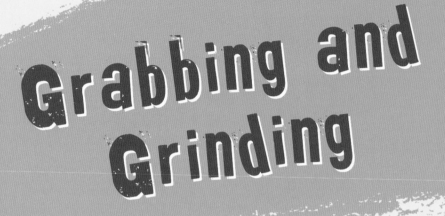

Grabbing and Grinding

A skater speeds down a halfpipe ramp. He glides up the other side. The skater reaches the top of the ramp. He sails high into the air.

The skater is high above the ramp. He reaches for his board to spin it in the air. This trick is called a varial.

BLAZER FACT

A halfpipe ramp is U-shaped.

Halfpipe ramp

The skater lands on his board. He speeds down the ramp. He is ready to do another trick.

BLAZER FACT

In 2002, skater Danny Way set a world record by jumping 18 feet, 3 inches (5.5 meters) above a ramp.

Skateboards

The deck is the main part of the skateboard. Most skateboard decks are made of wood.

Metal parts called trucks are under the deck. The trucks connect the wheels to the deck.

Truck

Wheel

Skateboard wheels are made of urethane. The wheels grip ramps, concrete bowls, and pavement.

BLAZER FACT

Years ago, skaters practiced in empty swimming pools.

Concrete bowl

Skatepark Diagram

Quarterpipe ramps

Coping

Fun box

Jump ramp

Slide rail

Tricks

Most skateboarding tricks begin with an ollie. Skaters step hard on the board's tail. The board then pops into the air.

Tail

Kickflip

Many skaters do street tricks.

Skaters do kickflips off benches.

They slide and grind along rails.

Slide

Grind

Coping

Skaters perform vert tricks off large halfpipe ramps. Skaters do spins, flips, and grabs. They grind on the coping.

Grab

safety

Falls are part of skateboarding. Helmets, elbow pads, and knee pads help protect skaters.

Some skaters build their own ramps. Others do grabs and grinds at skateparks. Safe skating places help skaters stay on the ramps, instead of on the sidelines.

BLAZER FACT

Each year, skateboarding injuries send about 50,000 skaters to U.S. hospital emergency rooms.

Grinding the coping

RAMP SURFACE
SKATELITE
WWW.SKATELITE.COM

Glossary

coping (KOH-ping)—a raised edge at the top of a skateboarding ramp

deck (DEK)—the main part of a skateboard

kickflip (KIK-flip)—a trick in which a skater spins the board with the feet

ollie (AH-lee)—a trick in which a skater steps on the board's tail to make the board pop into the air

truck (TRUHK)—the part of a skateboard that connects the wheels to the deck

urethane (YUR-uh-thayn)—a type of hard plastic used to make skateboard wheels

varial (VAIR-ee-uhl)—a trick that involves flipping the skateboard 180 degrees with the feet

Read More

Blomquist, Christopher. *Skateboarding in the X Games.* A Kid's Guide to the X Games. New York: PowerKids Press, 2003.

Horsley, Andy. *Skateboarding.* Radical Sports. Chicago: Heinemann, 2003.

Savage, Jeff. *Street Skating: Grinds and Grabs.* Skateboarding. Mankato, Minn.: Edge Books, 2005.

Internet Sites

FactHound offers a safe, fun way to find Internet sites related to this book. All of the sites on FactHound have been researched by our staff.

Here's how:

1. Visit *www.facthound.com*
2. Type in this special code **0736827307** for age-appropriate sites. Or enter a search word related to this book for a more general search.
3. Click on the **Fetch It** button.

FactHound will fetch the best sites for you!

Index